W9-AYO-657

Festivals *of the* World

MEXICO

Gareth Stevens Publishing
MILWAUKEE

DF BB mp

Written and edited by
ELIZABETH BERG

Designed by
LOO CHUAN MING

First published in North America in 1997 by
Gareth Stevens Publishing
1555 North RiverCenter Drive, Suite 201
Milwaukee, Wisconsin 53212 USA

For a free color catalog describing Gareth
Stevens' list of high-quality books and multimedia
programs, call
1-800-542-2595 (USA)
or 1-800-461-9120 (Canada).
Gareth Stevens Publishing's Fax: (414) 225-0377.
See our catalog, too, on the World Wide Web:
http://gsinc.com

© TIMES EDITIONS PTE LTD 1997
Originated and designed by
Times Books International
an imprint of Times Editions Pte Ltd
Times Centre, 1 New Industrial Road
Singapore 536196
Printed in Singapore

Library of Congress Cataloging-in-Publication Data:
Berg, Elizabeth, 1953–
Mexico / by Elizabeth Berg.
p. cm.—(Festivals of the world)
Includes bibliographical references (p. 27)
and index.
Summary: Describes the background and customs
associated with some of the important fiestas
celebrated in Mexico.
ISBN 0-8368-1686-2 (library binding)
1. Festivals—Mexico—Juvenile literature.
2. Mexico—Social life and customs—Juvenile
literature. [1. Festivals—Mexico. 2. Holidays—
Mexico. 3. Mexico—Social life and customs.]
I. Title. II. Series
GT4814.A2B47 1997
394.2'6972—dc20   96-9155

1 2 3 4 5 6 7 8 9 99 98 97

CONTENTS

13,95

It's Festival Time . . .

The word for "festival" or "party" in Spanish is *fiesta* [fee-AYS-tah]. Mexico has more festivals than any other Latin American country. There is a fiesta somewhere in Mexico on every day of the year.

Most fiestas include music and dancing and good things to eat. Children celebrate with a *piñata* full of candies. (Don't know what a *piñata* is?—find out on page 25.) Come along and join the party! It's festival time in Mexico . . .

Where's Mexico?

Mexico lies just south of the United States. Many years ago, the western part of the United States also belonged to Mexico, including California, Arizona, New Mexico, Colorado, Nevada, and Utah. The land of Mexico varies greatly. It ranges from volcanoes and snowy mountains to deserts and tropical rain forests. The capital, Mexico City, is one of the largest cities in the world.

This painting shows how Diego Rivera, a great Mexican artist, imagined the Aztec capital. The city was built in the middle of a lake. Food was grown in floating gardens.

A Mexican girl holds a stack of that favorite Mexican food, tortillas.

Who are the Mexicans?

Most Mexicans are **mestizo** [mess-TEE-zo], a mixture of Spanish and native peoples. After Columbus came to America, explorers moved out into the new land. Hernán Cortés came to Mexico in 1519 and found the **Aztecs** living there. They had a beautiful city where Mexico City stands today. Traders came from all around to their markets.

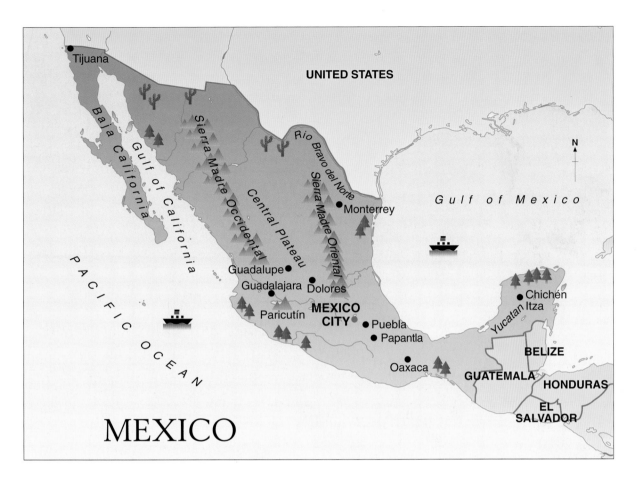

MEXICO

The Aztec leader, Montezuma, thought Cortés might be one of their gods returning. But he soon found that Cortés was only interested in getting their gold and silver. The Spanish conquered the Aztecs and made them work as slaves.

After a long time, the Spaniards and the native peoples mixed and created the mestizo people. Mexico today is also a mixture of Spanish and Aztec traditions.

The early people of Mexico built large pyramids like this one at Chichén Itza. Many of these pyramids are still standing.

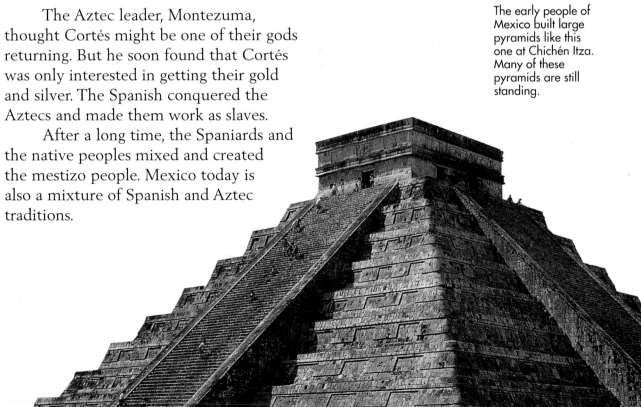

WHEN'S THE FIESTA?

SPRING

- ✪ **BIRTHDAY OF BENITO JUÁREZ**
- ✪ **HOLY WEEK AND EASTER**
- ✪ **LABOR DAY**
- ✪ **BATTLE OF PUEBLA** (Cinco de Mayo)

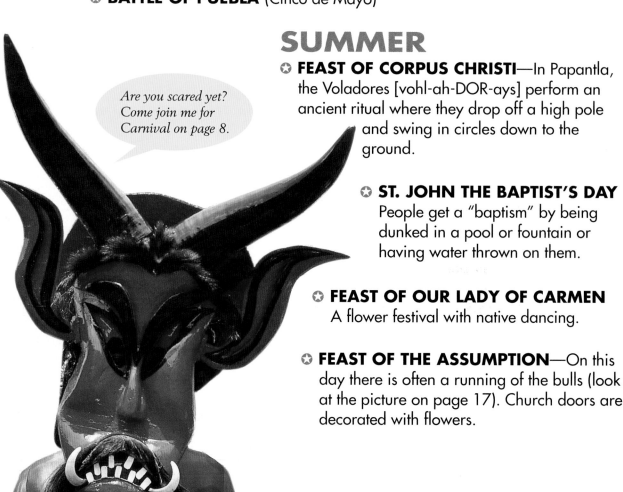

Are you scared yet? Come join me for Carnival on page 8.

SUMMER

- ✪ **FEAST OF CORPUS CHRISTI**—In Papantla, the Voladores [vohl-ah-DOR-ays] perform an ancient ritual where they drop off a high pole and swing in circles down to the ground.

- ✪ **ST. JOHN THE BAPTIST'S DAY** People get a "baptism" by being dunked in a pool or fountain or having water thrown on them.

- ✪ **FEAST OF OUR LADY OF CARMEN** A flower festival with native dancing.

- ✪ **FEAST OF THE ASSUMPTION**—On this day there is often a running of the bulls (look at the picture on page 17). Church doors are decorated with flowers.

Go ahead—make my day (the Day of the Dead, that is). Join me on page 22.

Ride on over to page 19 for Independence Day.

AUTUMN

- ✪ **INDEPENDENCE DAY**
- ✪ **DÍA DE LA RAZA** (Day of the Race)—The day when Columbus landed in the New World. Mexicans celebrate this day as the beginning of the mestizo people from the mixing of Spanish and native peoples.
- ✪ **DAY OF THE DEAD**
- ✪ **REVOLUTION DAY**—There is a big parade of athletes in Mexico City to celebrate the Mexican Revolution of 1910.

WINTER

- ✪ **FEAST OF THE VIRGIN OF GUADALUPE**
- ✪ **NAVIDAD** (Christmas) ✪ **NEW YEAR'S DAY**
- ✪ **EPIPHANY** (Three Kings Day)
- ✪ **ST. ANTHONY'S DAY**—Children put ribbons and flowers on their pets and take them to the church to be blessed.
- ✪ **DÍA DE LA CANDELARIA**—Candles and seeds for planting are blessed in the churches.
- ✪ **CARNIVAL**

Feliz Navidad! We're having a Christmas party on pages 24 and 25.

CARNIVAL AND EASTER

Mexican festivals are full of color and excitement. Probably the most exciting and colorful is Carnival. Carnival is celebrated in many Catholic countries. Catholics used to fast during the day for 40 days before Easter. This was called Lent. Before starting this long fast, people celebrated with a big festival. Today, Catholics don't generally fast for the entire time of Lent, but they still celebrate Carnival in many countries.

A day of surprises

Carnival is a time when anything can happen. As you walk down the street, you bump into people wearing masks and fantastic costumes. Fireworks explode all around. Musicians play tunes as they stroll along. There are always parades. Brightly decorated floats move down the main street carrying people in costumes.

These children are dressed up as Mexican soldiers for Carnival.

Different kinds of battles

Women and children sometimes have flower battles for Carnival. They line up and throw flowers at each other and at anyone else standing around.

Children also like to have egg battles. They blow out the eggs and fill the shells with confetti. Then the children form two lines. They walk past each other and try to break their eggs on each other's heads as they pass.

These people are dressed up as Spanish conquerors, called **conquistadores** [kon-kee-sta-DOR-ays]. Carnival is a time when people are expected to act in ways that are usually not allowed. A long time ago, the native peoples used Carnival as a chance to make fun of the Spanish. These costumes are now part of the tradition of Carnival.

Easter

Easter comes after the fasting time of Lent. It is an important holiday in Mexico. At this time, Mexicans think about Christ's sacrifice. There are special ceremonies at the church. Mexicans also celebrate with singing and dancing, and there are a lot of special foods to eat.

Above: On Good Friday, the day when Christ was crucified, Mexicans put on a play of his death. The drama takes place in the town plaza.

Right: These people are taking part in the Good Friday procession. Their costumes are a lot like the costumes worn at processions in Spain that have gone on for a long time. They wear hoods to show they are sorry for their sins.

Setting Judas on fire

A special Mexican Easter tradition is to hang a **papier-mâché** model of Judas, the person who betrayed Christ, from a balcony. Often he is made to look like someone people don't like. Strings of firecrackers are wound around the Judas and candles and toys are tied to it.

On Saturday morning at 10:00 a.m., the church bells start to ring, and the firecrackers are lit. As the firecrackers explode, they set the Judas figure on fire. The toys and candies fall, and children rush to grab the treats.

Firecrackers are dangerous, so these days the Judas figure is usually filled with candies and beaten until it breaks and the candies fall down.

Lighting the fireworks on a Judas figure for Easter in a small town in Mexico.

Think about this

Mexicans like to dress up as Spanish conquistadores for Carnival. Do you ever dress up like a famous person to poke fun at them? Have you seen other people do this for a festival? Do you ever dress up like people from history?

THE FEAST OF OUR LADY OF GUADALUPE

I f you were in Guadalupe, Mexico (Guadalupe is a little town in central Mexico. Find it on the map on page 5.) on December 12, you would see crowds of people going to the main square in front of the church. Let's follow them. There's music coming from the square. You can smell the tacos, tostadas, and tamales from the food stalls around the square. Now you can see the dancers with their feather headdresses. These are *conchero* [cone-CHAY-roh] dancers. *Conchero* comes from the word *concha*, which means "shell" in Spanish. These dancers wear bracelets of shells around their ankles. The shells make a rhythm as they dance.

Left: Boys dress up like **peasants** for the festival. They wear a *serape* [say-RAH-pay], which is a colorful blanket worn by peasants, and sandals and a false mustache. Or they might wear white pants and a white shirt with a mask. They are called *Dieguitos* [dee-ay-GEE-tohs], which means "Little Diegos." Who's Diego? Read the story on page 15.

Opposite: These conchero dancers are making a rhythm with their sticks.

A Long Walk

On the day of the fiesta, millions of people make a **pilgrimage** to Guadalupe to thank Our Lady of Guadalupe for answering their prayers. They come from all around. Some walk for days or ride their bicycles from far away to get there. Who's Our Lady of Guadalupe?

Below: Conchero dancers for the Feast of Our Lady of Guadalupe imitate the way the Aztecs used to dress for festivals. They wear feather headdresses, and bells and shells around their ankles.

Right: Climbing the steps to the Shrine of Our Lady of Guadalupe.

Listen to a story . . .

One morning in 1531 (that's 40 years after Columbus came to America), a poor peasant named Juan Diego was on his way to church when a lovely lady appeared before him. She had brown skin and was dressed like a Native Mexican. She told Juan that she was the Virgin Mary, and she asked him to tell the local bishop to build a church in her honor. When Diego told the bishop about this, he said Juan was crazy. The next day the Virgin appeared again, and Juan told her what the bishop said. She told him to pick some roses from a special spot. Roses had never grown in this spot before, but Juan went and found roses growing there. He wrapped them in his serape and brought them to the bishop. When he opened the serape, there was a picture of the Virgin printed on the inside. The bishop then built the shrine and put the serape in it. You can still see Juan's serape in the church today.

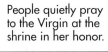

People quietly pray to the Virgin at the shrine in her honor.

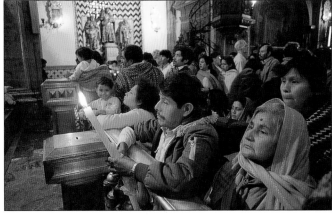

Think about this

The Festival of Our Lady of Guadalupe is on the same day as an older festival for an Aztec goddess. Often Christian festivals take the place of earlier festivals. When people became Christian, they changed their old festivals to new ones, but they kept many of the old customs. Do you know who gave out presents before Santa Claus? (Give up? Look on page 26.)

A very Mexican saint

Mexicans are very fond of the Virgin of Guadalupe. Many people come every year to ask her for favors or thank her for helping them. You can see her picture all over when you go to Mexico, just like the one on this page. Mexicans feel that the Virgin showed she cared about them by making herself look like a Native Mexican.

They feel she is one of them.

CELEBRATING MEXICO

There are some holidays when Mexicans remember people who made a difference to their country. On March 21, Mexicans celebrate the birthday of their best-loved leader, Benito Juárez. Juárez was a Zapotec (that's one of the many groups of Native Mexicans). His parents died when he was three years old. He was poor when he was young, but he worked hard to get ahead. In 1861, he became the first native president of Mexico. Juárez always worked to help the poor people of Mexico, especially the native peoples. He freed them from working on the haciendas, large farms where they worked almost as slaves.

A portrait of Benito Juárez.

Left: Another holiday celebrates Benito Juárez: the Cinco de Mayo. "Cinco de Mayo" means May 5th in Spanish, and that is the day when Benito Juárez and his army beat the French at the Battle of Puebla, when the French were trying to take over Mexico. To remember this day, Mexicans dress up in costumes and pretend to have a battle. Of course, the Mexican army wins.

Opposite: A running of the bulls. A bull is let loose in the main street of town, and brave people get a chance to try their skill in bullfighting. This is a popular part of many Mexican festivals.

Do Mexicans have an Independence Day?

Mexico celebrates its independence on September 16th every year. That isn't really the day Mexico became independent. It's the day when it all started.

A painting of Father Hidalgo by the famous Mexican painter, Diego Rivera. On Independence Day, people remember brave Father Hidalgo, who started the movement that led to Mexico's independence.

A long time ago . . .

Father Miguel Hidalgo y Costilla was a priest in the little town of Dolores. He and his friends felt, as did many other Mexicans, that they were treated unfairly by Spain. They thought Mexico should be independent, so they planned a revolution. On September 16th, Father Hidalgo went into the church and started ringing the bells. When the people came, he told them about his plans. At the end he shouted, *"Viva México! Viva la independencia!"* That means "Long live Mexico! Long live independence!" The townspeople took whatever weapons they could find and marched with him. More and more people joined them along the way. This was the start of the Mexican Revolution.

An Independence Day parade.

Think about this

Mexico is a mixture of many traditions. On holidays, many Mexican women wear an embroidered white blouse with a full red and green skirt decorated with sequins and beads. This dress is called the *China Poblana,* which means "Chinese woman from Puebla." The story goes that the China Poblana was an Indian princess who was brought to Mexico. She married a Chinese man and became known for her good works. This dress was her favorite costume, and it has become the favorite of Mexican women.

What happens on Independence Day?

At 11:00 p.m. on September 16th every year, the president of Mexico steps out on the balcony of the National Palace and cries, *"Viva México! Viva la independencia!"* The crowd echoes back, *"Viva México! Viva la independencia!"* At the same time, the mayors of all the towns in Mexico do the same. Then everyone throws confetti, and fireworks are set off in red, white, and green—the colors of the Mexican flag.

Charros are skillful riders who perform daring feats with a horse and lasso. Going to see charros perform is a favorite way to celebrate Independence Day.

19

THE DAY OF THE DEAD

A group of people in long robes are marching down the main street. They are carrying a coffin. Suddenly, the coffin opens and a skeleton pops out.

It's November 1st in Mexico, and this is a procession for the Day of the Dead. People everywhere dress as ghosts, skeletons, or witches. The markets are all full of toy skeletons and candies that look like little skulls. Children eat skulls with their name on the forehead.

Above: Chocolate skulls on sale at a market.

Opposite: A woman puts the finishing touches on an altar decorated with flowers and candles.

What is the Day of the Dead?

For Christians around the world, November 1st is All Saints' Day. The Mexicans call this day the Day of the Dead. Mexicans believe that the spirits of people who have died return to the world of the living at this time.

Waiting for the dead

People prepare by going to the graves of their relatives. They sweep and clean the grave and lay flowers on it. They put out the dead person's favorite foods and drinks, and candles and incense to lead the spirit back. Then they keep watch by the grave all night, waiting for the spirits to come back. The souls of children who have died return on the night of October 31. They are called the *muertitos chicos* [mwer-TEE-toes CHEE-kohs], the "dear little dead ones." People leave out toys, cakes, and hot chocolate to sweeten their return. The next night, the adults return. After feeding the dead, everyone returns to the house and eats a big meal to celebrate life.

Music for the ghosts

Sometimes people even provide music for the returning spirits, so you might find a **mariachi** band playing in the corner of the graveyard. Mariachi bands started about 100 years ago. Mariachi is typically Mexican music.

This skeleton is dressed up in the costume of a soldier in the Mexican Revolution. Look at his *sombrero*, the big hat with flowers embroidered on it. These hats are known all over the world as Mexican hats.

People talk while waiting for the dead to return. They've decorated the graves with marigolds and candles. The Aztecs believed marigolds were the flowers of the dead. They also took time to remember the dead during the month of November, but they had a whole "month of the dead."

Mariachis wear tight black pants and short black jackets with silver studs on the sides. They may also wear large sombreros. There are usually four men in a band, some playing guitar or violin, some horns.

Think about this
The eve of the Day of the Dead is celebrated in the United States as Halloween. Do you see any differences between Halloween and the Day of the Dead? Any things that are the same?

NAVIDAD

The Spanish word for "Christmas" is *Navidad* [nah-vee-DAD]. Mexicans wish each other "Feliz Navidad" [fay-LEES nah-vee-DAD] around Christmastime. Mexican children do many of the same things for Christmas that children do in the United States. They decorate Christmas trees, and they visit Santa Claus. Traditionally, they get their presents on January 6th, the day when the three wise men brought gifts to the infant Jesus. They leave their shoes by the door along with water for the wise men's camels. In the morning, the water is gone and the shoes are full of presents. Today they often get gifts on Christmas, too.

Children getting their picture taken with Santa Claus. Have you ever done this?

Looking for shelter

Mexicans also have some Christmas traditions that Americans don't, like *posada* [poh-SAH-dah] processions. *Posada* means "rest," and this tradition relives Mary and Joseph's search for a place to rest. Groups of children go from door to door around their neighborhood. Two of the children are dressed up like Mary and Joseph. At each house, they sing, "I am tired. I beg for rest." From inside the house other children sing, "Go away, go away, there is no room." They keep on until they get to a house where they are let in. There they have a Christmas party.

Children in a posada procession with a real donkey.

How to have a piñata party

Piñatas [pee-NYAH-tas] are made of either clay or papier-mâché covered with curls of tissue. They are filled with candies and, sometimes, small toys. Piñatas come in many different shapes, from traditional Christmas stars to Batman figures.

At a party, the piñata is hung from a tree just out of reach. An adult holds the rope to move the piñata up and down. A child is blindfolded. He or she takes a bat and tries to hit the piñata. Each child takes a turn until someone breaks the piñata, and the candies spill out on the ground. Then everyone runs to grab as many candies as they can.

Trying to break the piñata at a party. Piñatas are popular at Christmas parties, birthdays, and all kinds of fiestas.

THINGS FOR YOU TO DO

If you were in Mexico on Independence Day, you might celebrate by having a cup of Mexican Hot Chocolate with *galletas* [gah-YAY-tahs]—those are Mexican cookies. Look for some in a Mexican market, or try making your own by adding red, white, and green sprinkles on sugar cookies.

Sing a cockroach song

You could also try singing "La Cucaracha" [lah koo-kah-RAH-cha]. You may know the song already, but did you know that it's about a cockroach? And did you know that it's also about Pancho Villa, who was a hero of the Mexican Revolution? The song says that the prettiest girl to travel with Pancho Villa was a cockroach with no legs. (Sounds like the soldiers didn't have many girlfriends, doesn't it?) Here are the words in Spanish and English, with guides to help you sing it in Spanish.

Make Mexican Hot Chocolate
Mix these in a cup:
1 teaspoon cocoa
3 teaspoons sugar
⅓ cup powdered milk
½ teaspoon cinnamon
Fill the cup with hot water and stir. Put 1 tablespoon whipped cream on top.

Or, when you're in a Mexican market, look for bars of Mexican chocolate and a *molinillo* [moh-lee-NEE-yo]—that's a wooden beater that you twirl between your palms to break up the chocolate.

Answer to page 15: Before Christian times, the pagan god Odin visited earth around the end of December to reward good and punish evil. Saint Nicholas, later Santa Claus, took over his duties.

La Cucaracha

Things to look for in your library

Ashes for Gold: A Folktale from Mexico. Katherine Maitland (Mondo, 1995).

Beneath the Stone: A Mexican Zapotec Tale. Bernard Wolf (Orchard Books, 1994).

Benito Juarez: President of Mexico. Frank De Varona (Millbrook Press, 1993).

Cooking the Mexican Way. Rosa Coronado (First Avenue Editions, 1992).

Discovering the Music of Latin America (video).

Look What We've Brought You from Mexico. Phyllis Shalant (Julian Messner, 1992).

Los Mariachis: An Introduction to Mexican Mariachi Music (book and cassette).

The Piñata Maker. George Ancona (Harcourt Brace, 1994).

Postcards from Mexico. Helen Arnold (Raintree, 1995).

MAKE AN AZTEC SHIELD

M ake your own Aztec shield like the one the *conchero* dancers carry in the Festival of Our Lady of Guadalupe. You can choose a Mexican picture or make your own drawing.

This shield is done using yarn, in the style of yarn paintings made by the Huichol people, who live on the Pacific Coast of Mexico. If you don't want to use yarn, you can just paint your picture on the shield.

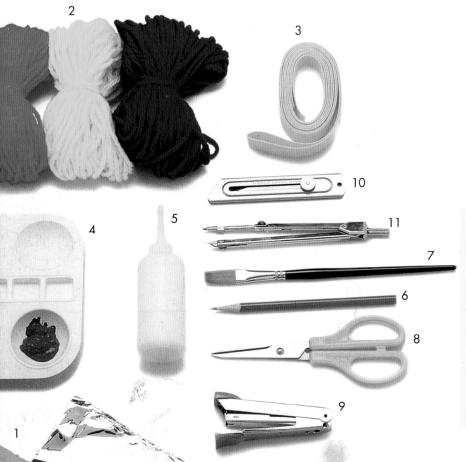

You will need:
1. Cardboard and gold foil paper
2. Balls of heavy yarn
3. Elastic
4. Tempera paint
5. Glue
6. Pencil
7. Brushes
8. Scissors
9. Stapler
10. Xacto knife
11. Compass

2 Cut the cardboard in a circle. Cut slits in the shield and put elastic through them. Cut the elastic and staple it in the back so that it fits over your arm.

1 Draw the outline of a plant, animal, person, or other shape in the center of the cardboard square.

3 Paint around your drawing with the color you want your shield to be.

4 Put glue on the outline and press yarn into the glue, one or two strands at a time. Spread glue inside the shape and press yarn into it. Use one or two strands of yarn at a time and follow the shape of the outline. Use different colors.

5 Cut a circle from the foil to fit around the edge of the shield and glue it in place. Cut it to make a fringe. Make a border by spreading glue around the edges of the shield. Press yarn along the edges, making different colored stripes.

MAKE GUACAMOLE

Favorite foods at festivals are tamales, tostadas, and tacos. These are all made with tortillas, which are like thin corn pancakes. Mexicans eat tortillas with almost every meal. Mexican food is mostly made of different variations of corn, beans, and rice. These three together along with some fruits and vegetables make a healthy diet.

Another favorite festival food is guacamole [wah-kah-MOE-lay]. You can make guacamole easily at home. Here's how.

You will need:
1. 2 ripe avocados
2. Half a small onion
3. 2-3 sprigs fresh cilantro
4. 1 jalapeño pepper (if you like it spicy)
5. 2 tomatoes
6. 2 tablespoons lemon juice
7. Salt
8. Spoon
9. Fork
10. Bowl
11. Knife
12. Measuring spoons

1 Cut the avocados in half, take out the seeds, and scoop out the avocado.

2 Put the avocado in a bowl and mash it up with a fork.

3 Chop up the onion, cilantro, pepper, and tomatoes. Add them all to the avocado.

4 Add the lemon juice and a little salt until it tastes right. Mix it well. Dip in your tortilla chips and eat!

GLOSSARY

Aztecs, 4 — People who lived in Mexico when the Spanish came.

charro, 19 — A person who performs tricks on horseback for a rodeo.

conchero, 12 — A dancer who wears shells around his ankles.

conquistador, 9 — A person who wins a war with someone else.

fiesta, 3 — A festival or party.

mariachi, 22 — A type of music from Mexico.

mestizo, 4 — People who are part Spanish and part native.

papier-mâché, 11 — Made of layers of paper dipped in flour water and dried.

peasant, 12 — A poor farmer.

pilgrimage, 14 — A trip to a holy place.

piñata, 25 — A papier-mâché or clay figure filled with candies.

serape, 12 — A colorful blanket worn by peasants.

sombrero, 22 — A hat.

INDEX